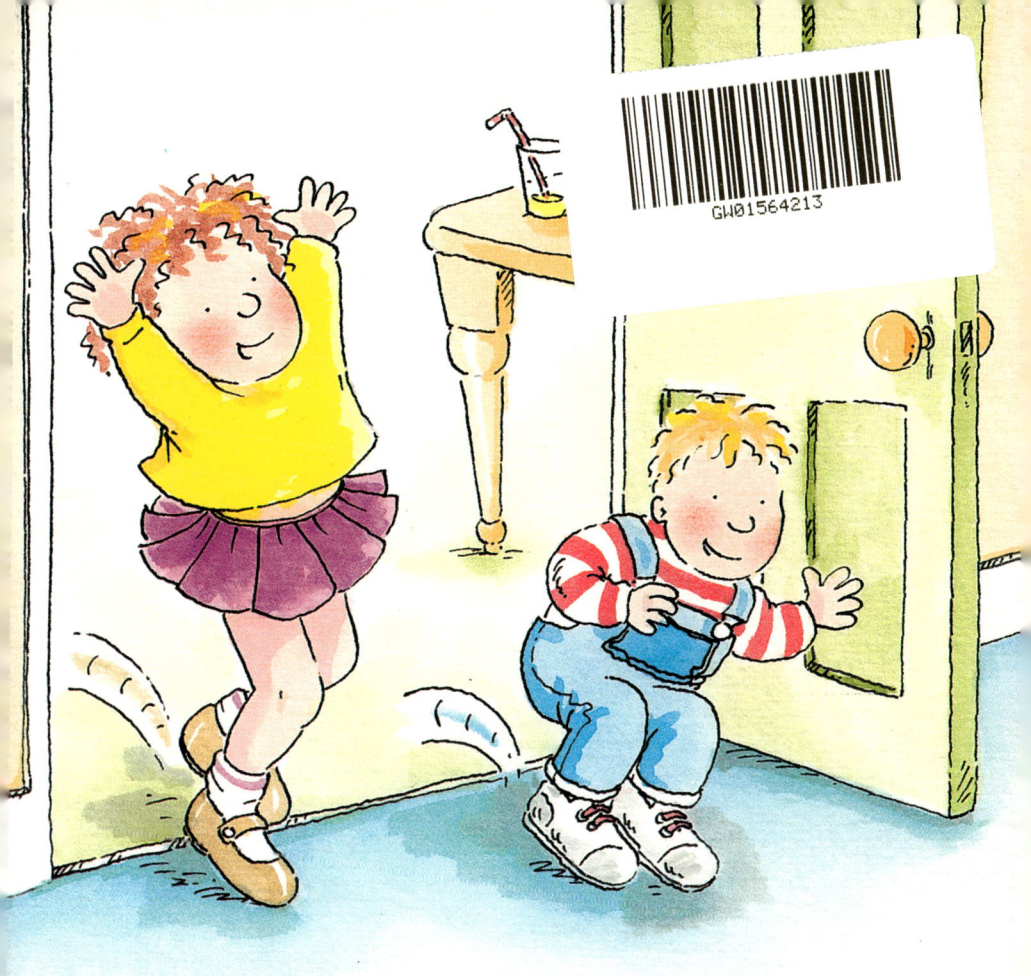

Jump, jump,

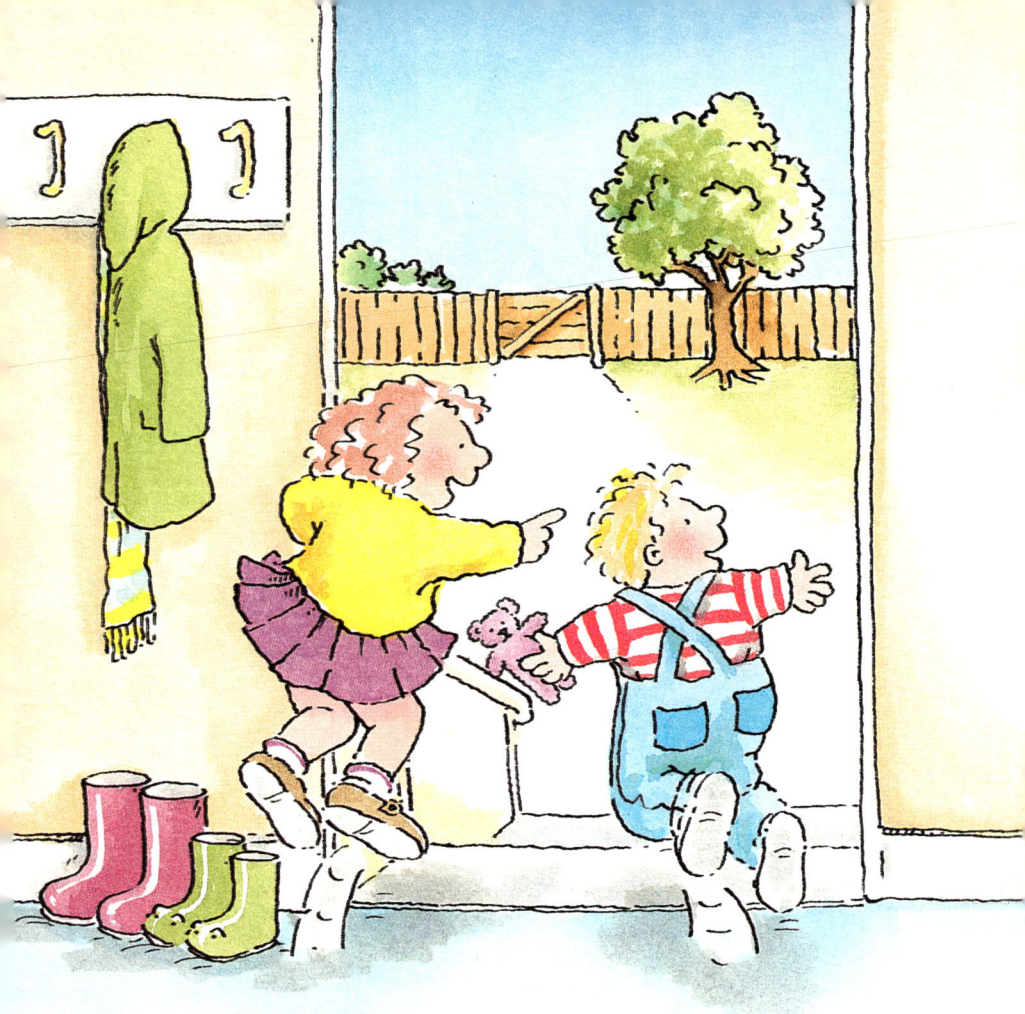

jump, jump.

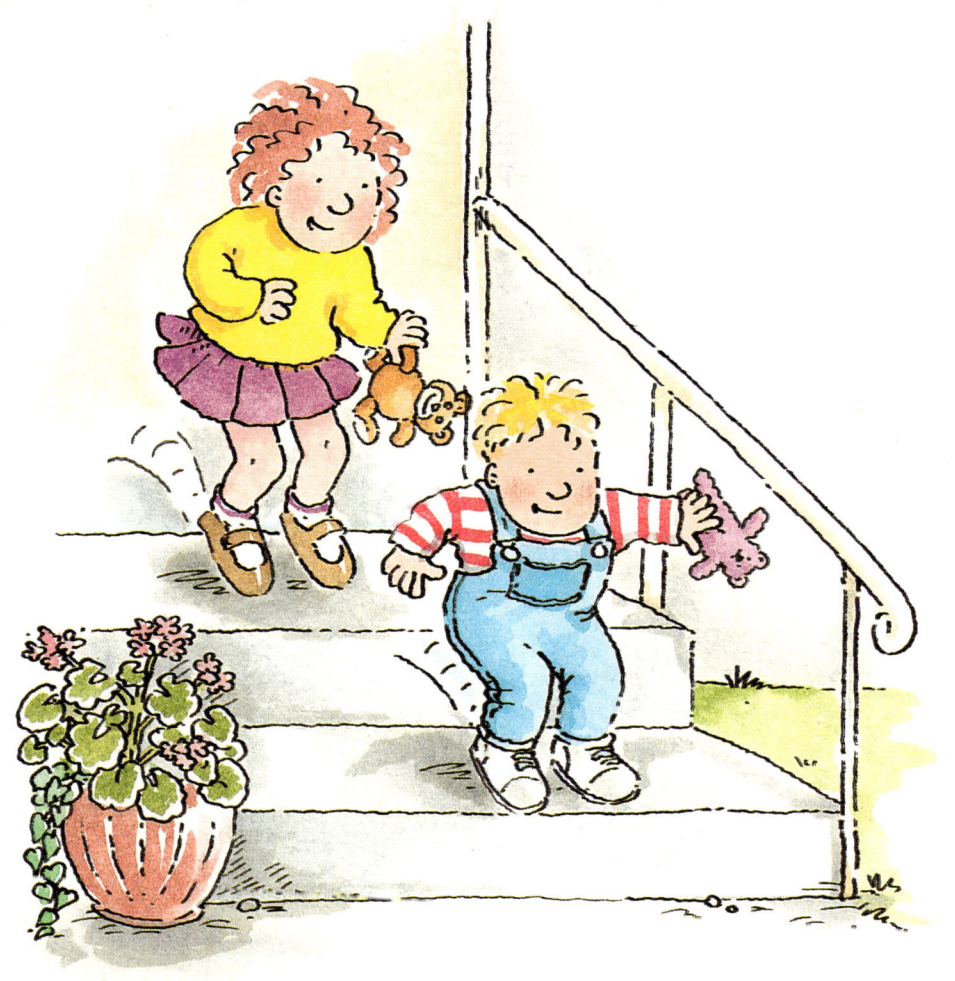

We're jumping with our bears.

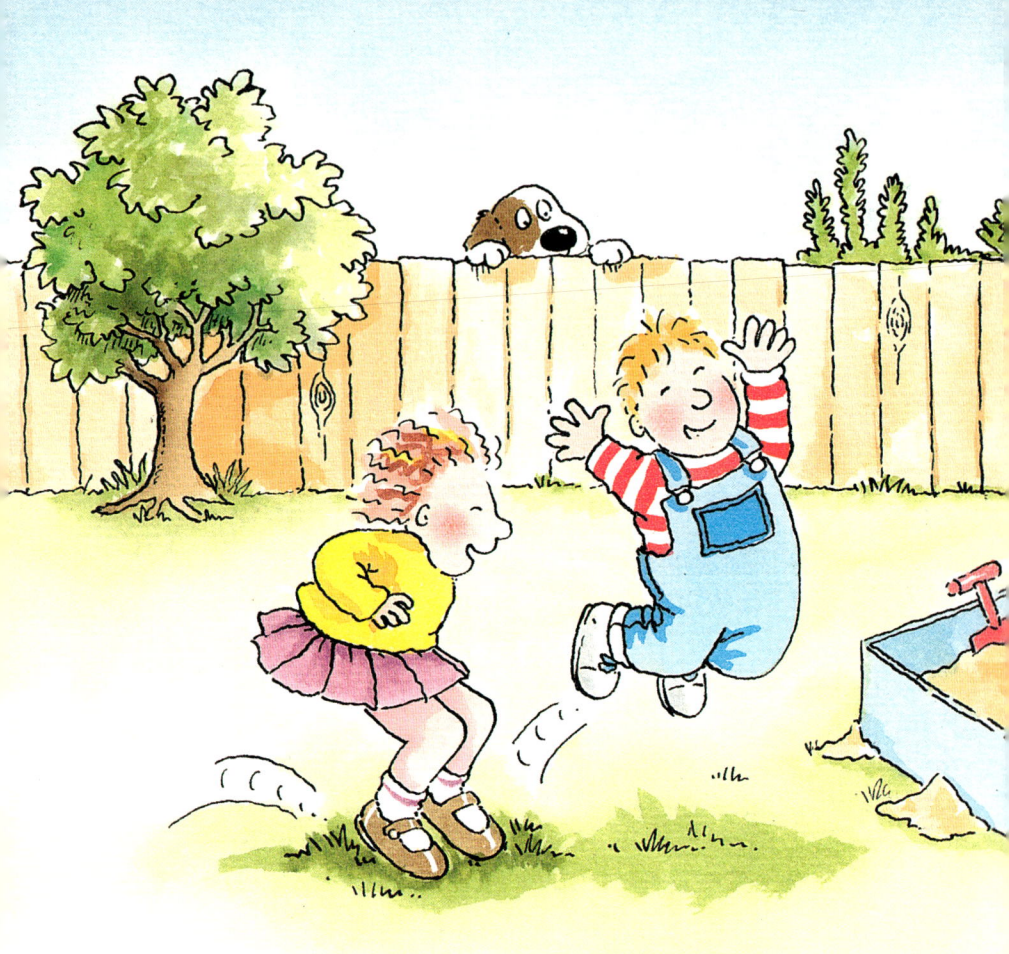

Jump, jump, jump, jump.

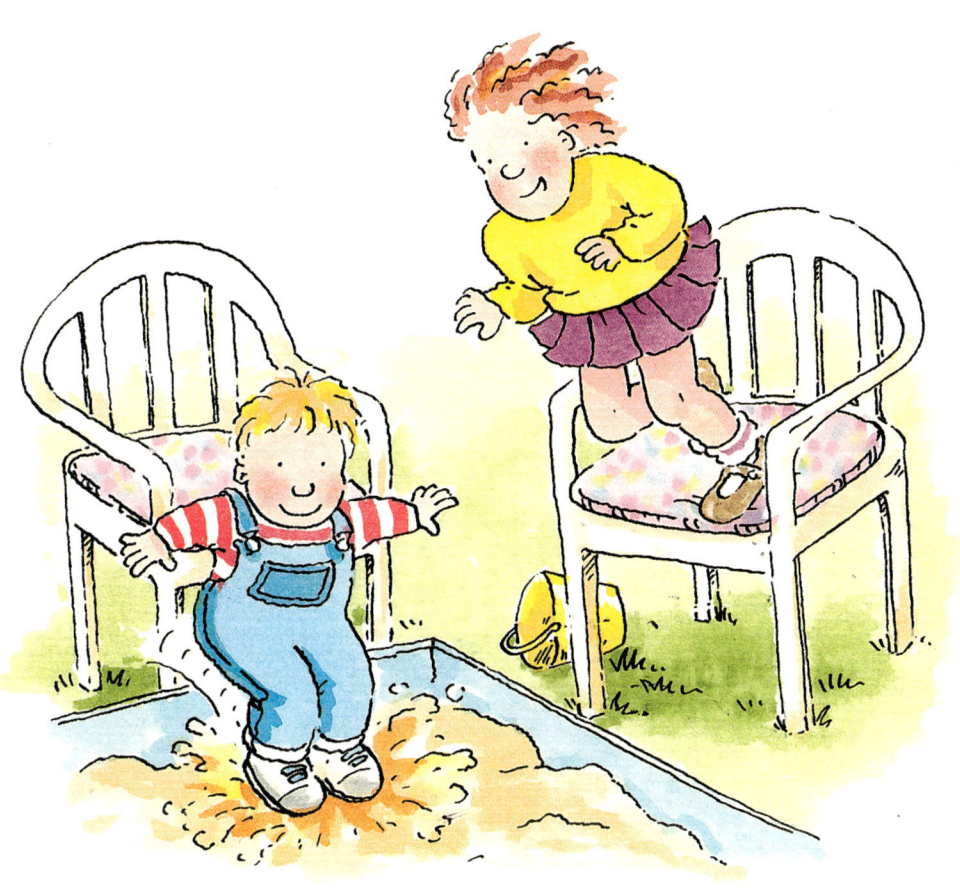

We're jumping off the chairs.

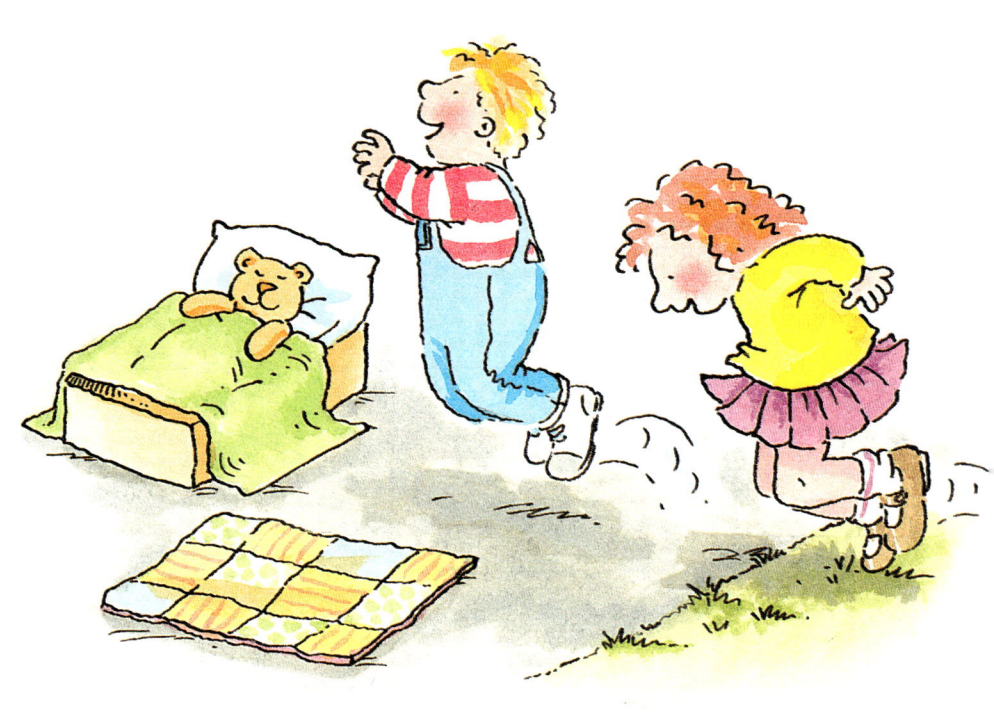

Jump, jump, jump, jump.

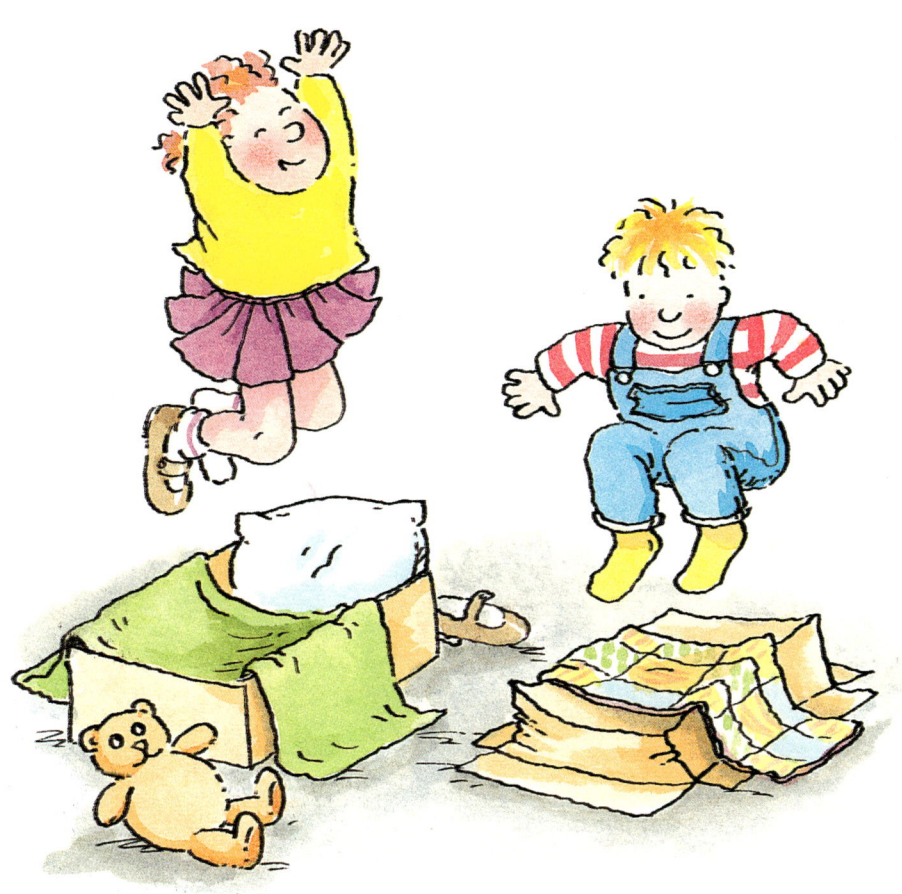

We're jumping on our beds.

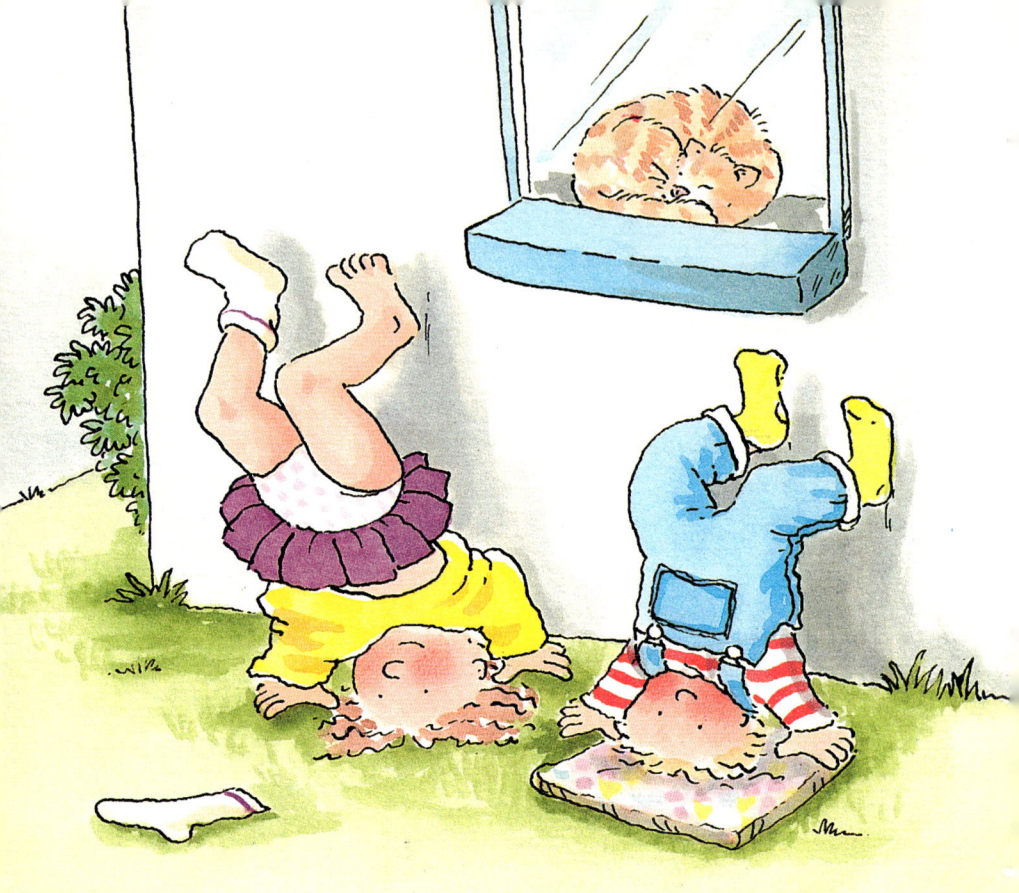

Now we've finished jumping and we're standing on our heads.